# Passive Income Ideas

Discover How to Create Multiple
Streams of Income Using Digital
Automation

## _For True Financial Freedom_

Max Armin

# Passive Income Ideas

*Discover How To Create Multiple Streams of Income Using Digital Automation For True Financial Freedom.*

Published By:
Dana Publishing, LLC.
Mentor, Ohio

# Table of Contents

# Introduction to Passive Income

Typically, we work to earn money. But we can make money work for us.

What is the real goal with creating passive income?

**..*FREEDOM***

- Location freedom, to live or work where you want.

- Freedom to do and be whatever you want.

- Freedom to follow your true passions and creative endeavors.

- Freedom to see the world.

- Freedom to not have to worry about common living expenses.

Passive income is a means of making money that may require little or no-maintenance work once it hits the ground running. Some passive income ideas such as online courses, ebooks may demand a commitment to build and launch. However, once the final product is released in the market, you can step back and maintain a decent amount of cash flow, for whatever your goal is.

Still, it is wrong to think that passive income doesn't require any work. There's nothing like 100% passive income. Even with rental property investments, you will still have to manage the manager that is managing your properties. In other words, there's always some time involved even after launching your business and achieving a stable platform of income and success. But who cares? The reality is that we have it made today, with the proliferation of the Internet, ANYONE can set up an international business and sell widgets or services online. The smart ones figure out ways to automate it after achieving some level of success using low-cost virtual assistants, software, lead generation and automations.

Regardless of how much money and time you have, there's at least one passive income idea that will work for you. In this book, we walk your though passive income ideas that will help you earn money part-time.

I personally found my passive income model from real estate investing combined with an online business. I started out by flipping investor properties locally where I lived through a website I created and advertised through SEO and Google PPC Search ads. I was able to automate the business when I hired a property manager and was able to set up lead automation and management systems.

This allowed me to step out of the management process and run the business in a very minimalist manner, even at multiple six-figures a year. I eventually transitioned over to a 100 % digital model and it continues to grow to this day.

There are numerous ways anyone can find one business or niche to create passive income from, or even possibly combine several ideas to create a new one. Everyone has some sort of edge or unique talent, skill or knowledge to do this.

**People place value on skill and knowledge in a wide variety of hobbies and are ready to pay for that knowledge.**

# Chapter 1: Introduction to Passive Income

## What Passive Income Means

Passive income refers to earnings extracted from enterprises that a person is not actively involved constantly. This can include rental property investment, forex trading, online businesses and many more. Passive income is income that is not proportional to the time you commit to earning it. This means that "time in" does not equal "money out." In simple terms, you eventually earn more than the effort you put in.

### Breaking down passive income

There are three types of income: portfolio income, active income, and passive income. In recent years, the term passive income has been loosely used. Typically, it has been used to refer to money that is being earned regularly with little or no effort on the side of the person earning it. Some of the popular forms of passive income include peer-to-peer lending, dividend stocks, and real estate. The proponents of passive income tend to good supporters of work-from-home and be-your-own boss lifestyle.

The types of income that is often linked with this include profits on interest, retirement pay, online work, and capital gains. Although these tasks go hand in hand with the popular definition of passive income, it doesn't match the technical description outlined in the IRS.

Passive income, when applied as a technical term, it can be said to be "net rental income" or "income from a business which the taxpayer does not materially take part, "and in some cases involve self-charged interest. It proceeds to say that passive income "does not include portfolio, investment income, or salaries."

If you search the web today for ideas on passive income, you'll find a large number of posts that try to describe different methods for one to use to generate this type of income. But, what you'll come to learn is that most of those posts that talk about the different methods to make passive income, such as real estate, aren't passive.

## So what's the truth?

There are few passive ideas for making income. Even when it comes to real estate income, there is a cost involved. Do you want to launch a blog to make passive income? These models are proven but the upfront work can be intense too get it to the passive phase, are you willing to do this?

Any amount of passive takes time to build since you have to also build an effective audience for long term growth in whatever niche you're in before significant cash flow becomes constant and regular. However, don't think this will take years, because of the technologies now available to almost anyone now plus the highly targeted online audience and markets you have access to, this can be achieved in 3 to 12 months, depending on how hard you work.

There are multiple ways both slow and fast to make passive income. But, before you can jump in to explore the different types of passive income, it is important that you fully understand what they are.

The one thing that differentiates active income from passive income is that active income requires regular input of time to generate revenues whereas the latter doesn't.

A large percent of the world is involved in active income activities. In other words, they actively trade time for money, plain and simple. So if these people stop working, then they stop earning. But you want to put this to a stop. What happens when you fall ill or get involved in an accident, and you can't work? Clearly, it will be difficult to make money. With passive income, it is possible to make money whether you're working or not, but this takes a massive effort and time.

To create a decent amount of passive income, you have to be ready to invest a lot of time and money upfront, that is the key here, more so time than money too.

**Why is passive income important to people?**

People generally want to make a lot of money with less effort and more freedom and time to pursue other interests. Yes, it's interesting to have a lot of time to do what you want to, but these aren't the only benefits of passive income.

You're going to learn why passive income is so important, and the reasons why everyone can have passive income in today's digital economy, or even be actively involved in passive income.

You'll have a bright, more stable retirement life versus those depending on savings, or a pension.

Retirement planning is a big problem for most people, and it shouldn't be, but when most people don't have enough knowledge about new wealth creation and think that saving money is the only means they have to plan for retirement. The savings plan does not appear to work anymore, judging by statistics.

Savings isn't a reliable means because it creates a vulnerable side to sudden changes in both personal life and the general economy.

A recent study discovered that 70 % of American baby boomers felt that their retirement saving wasn't enough.

That's quite shocking and scary static to have 70% of a generation feel insecure about their retirement. An age that's the wealthiest compared to all the rest of us.

The fact is, many of us have been taught to save money as a means for retirement simply, and that should be enough to support us in our golden years if we work long enough and save enough.

But even if you save wisely and work until the recommended age, most people don't know that unexpected expenses often occur as you grow old, and really they are almost guaranteed to occur.

Most people underestimate how much they need to save. The state pensions around the world are on the chopping block. The government treasurers are becoming smaller, and budgets are being slashed. This is bad news for anyone who is hoping to rely on the state to provide for them in the old age.

As the lifespan of people is getting longer, most countries are choosing to increase the retirement age to qualify for a pension.

Yes, we're living longer, but that doesn't imply that we need to work for longer.

Why should someone what to work for more years and pay a lot of tax only to receive a smaller pension in return?

**So, when you create passive income, you'll be creating Cashflow.**

Cashflow is unique from savings because you're receiving a certain amount regularly. There's something that you'll be receiving, and it's not different from getting a paycheck. The only exception is that you won't be actively working. That is the reason is a safe retirement plan.

### Having the right mindset

Everyone loves to be rich. But why is that not the case? The truth is that most people don't make up their minds to achieve the goals they desire. They may not like their current situation, but they are just comfortable with it. And nothing is worst than being comfortable in a current situation when you are not happy but are settling at the same time with your reality. The secret is to develop a wealth mindset.

### 1. Concentrate on what you want to achieve and go for it

Most people fear to acknowledge that they want something and lay down the right steps to look for it. When you've something that you want to achieve don't say that "I could never actually do that," but think like "I could do that and I will do that." If you want to be a millionaire, you must play to win but not give up. For that reason, it is vital to becoming assertive and sincere to yourself. These ideas are very simple but this is how it works. Most people try and give it "a shot" but give up way, way too soon. We have all done it, started a project, spent money, didn't see immediate results that were favorable, and gave up.

If you had kept pushing through and re-asserting your goal and keeping focused, the goal would have been achieved.

## 2. Remain goal-oriented

Every successful entrepreneur has a goal that he works towards. This means that you can't accomplish something when you don't have a clear goal set. Unless you're a lottery winner, who becomes a millionaire overnight. But even before they play the lottery, they've set their goals to win the most significant price. While you set your goals, it is important to remain realistic. Don't set goals that it will take you 100 years to achieve; you'll eventually lose the grip of chasing after this goal. But if you can set goals that are achievable, with time, you'll finally accomplish it. The point is not to aim to become rich quickly because that way you will never be.

## 3. The money for investing should not be confused with money for spending.

For you to become a millionaire, you must know how to save. You need to understand that the true value of money lies in investing. Becoming your own boss is the path to becoming a millionaire. Make it your choice to invest money and reduce any unnecessary spending.

### 4. Don't stop learning

The best gift that you can reward yourself is to invest in yourself. Finishing school doesn't mean the end of learning. Successful people, never stop learning. For you to realize success, you must be knowledgeable about every concept about passive income and money management. The only way you can increase your knowledge is by reading books. Look for books written by millionaires, invest your time reading books and you'll develop the same mindset as that of millionaires.

### 5. Think big

Although it's advised to start with small goals, having the right mindset requires that you've big goals in mind. A big goal could be a business idea that you want to set up, make millions of dollars, and many more.

## What Passive income is not

Few things are attractive than passive income. What is more interesting than making more money without having to sweat a lot. When you read headlines that talk about how the founder of Amazon earns over $230, 000 per second, it's normal to start thinking about how you can earn that money when you're not working.

However, to generate income through passive income isn't that simple as some people say. To identify how you can make a constant flow of cash requires a lot of effort and commitment. You need to be willing to dedicate your time and capital in the right fields.

If you've made your mind to generate income through passive means, you should not believe the following myths.

### 1. Passive income allows you to "set and forget" your revenue streams

This is one of the dangerous myths spread about passive income.

Everyone loves the idea of not working after creating an online store or blog. But, that is not simple. Why? Even after setting up your blog, visitors will expect fresh content regularly. If you're going to sit back and think that you are going to make a passive income after setting up your blog or online store, you'll be shocked. If you don't do anything to grab your readers and stay on the industry, your passive income will quickly deplete. Even if you appoint a team of experts to help you out on tasks, you will need to supervise them. You'll also need to enhance your idea so that it can stay relevant. So don't be cheated, passive income will always demand an active presence, nothing like you make money while sleeping.

### 2. You just need a single weekend to start

It's easy to think that anyone can set up a blog or any other type of passive income in a single weekend. The fact is, creating a passive income stream that will deliver the best and long-lasting results requires a lot of research and work before you even make a single penny.

Even something simple like launching a blog will require extensive planning and in-depth research. You'll need to learn more about your audience. In short, you'll not manage to do everything on a single weekend. You must be ready to commit the time to learn the challenges associated with your idea and put the right effort to get it right.

### 3. A solid source of income is what you require

This is another myth about passive income. It is impossible to generate all the money you need with only a single source of the stream. This is like putting all your eggs in one basket. It will always crumple down. A trader who puts all the stock market investments into a single company may either become rich or lose all his money if the prices fall.

It's better to diversify your market so that you can spread the risk, especially when you know that the following revenue streams are going to replace your current job.

For instance, bloggers that have low web traffic may apply everything from affiliate links and sell their own products to freelance writing services and online courses to create extra income. By multiplying revenue streams, there's a better opportunity of earning enough to support the needs.

## 4. You need a business idea to make good money

When you read about passive income, it's easy to be caught up with the idea that you must become an entrepreneur or purchase a property. However, this isn't the case. Most people make all the passive income they require by just putting money in savings and retirement accounts.

Although the following accounts may not appear lucrative, they act as a lower-risk solution for those that want to have enough money to support their plans. Despite this, most investors advise that you need to expect a 5 percent return on investment is coming from your retirement accounts every year. That may not sound much, but as you always add to these accounts over time, the growth can be considerable. By saving a little extra every month can prove a big difference in the long run.

## Create passive income in the right way

Pursuing a dream of generating passive income isn't always easy—but it's far from achievable.

Whether you want to bring stability to your business or find the best way of financing your retirement, by avoiding these common misconceptions will go hand-in-hand to help you reach your goals. Success is near than you may imagine.

# Taking Massive Action

## How to create passive income

The first step to creating a passive income stream is to build a personal inventory and begin to identify your real goals, motivations, weaknesses, and strengths a little better.

- Why do you want to have a source of passive income?

- Will a source of passive income stream make your life appear differently? If so, how?

- How much money do you require to become financially free?

- How can you handle failure? Are you able to pick up after defeat and rebuild differently?

- What is the reason to postpone and leave projects before you attain the goal?

- What is the level of commitment to projects in the past? Especially, those projects that have snatched time from the things you used to enjoy doing?

- What are your weaknesses? What are your strengths?

- Are you ready to spend hours in front of a computer?

- Do you like communicating with people?

Your dedication and energy will be different with time. You tend to do well in some tasks and subjects, but not others. It is important to dive deep in the brain cells and try to understand more about yourself, what is it that you want and why do you want it. This type of knowledge is the first step towards getting ready for success. Use your opportunities wisely and eliminate your weaknesses. Most projects fail because most people don't understand themselves and their real purpose.

**Time and money**

After the tough process, then comes the less important but, more objective part. In this stage, you need to decide how much money, and time you want to commit. There are three methods that you can use to create passive income:

1. By investing in the capital upfront

2. By investing in the time upfront

3. By investing time and capital upfront.

The choice is always easy when you already know the capital and time you can invest.

**Make a choice and research**

By having a clear response to the previous section will make the process of choosing and researching your future stream of income easy. You know what types of assets that will have the biggest chances of success for your particular weaknesses, resources, and strengths. Find something that you're passionate about and identify whether these passions can be transformed into a passive income asset. If you fail to remember anything, look for the traditional passive income assets and turn them yours. Be innovative. When defining your goals, it can be a good thing to research similar projects and identify the risks and the rate of success that you can gain from this passive income asset.

It is hard to achieve success by a sudden flight; success is the result of consistency and dedication. Rather than search for the fast return investment to begin, search for the investment that you're ready to hold onto, no matter the surrounding situations.

**What type of passive income would you prefer to gain from your projects?**

There are eight types of capital as listed below:

- Financial capital
- Intellectual capital
- Cultural capital
- Material capital
- Social capital
- Experiential capital
- Living capital

## Setting goals

When it comes to setting goals, the most important thing is to understand where you want to arrive, if you have the mindset and determination, you will need to look for a way to reach there. Your goals should be milestones for your general goal. Each of the following milestones will assist you in generating the confidence and important attitude to arrive in the next stage. Divide the objectives into sub-goals, stick to your commitment and develop the fun in the process. Some roads may lead to other discoveries and purposes.

## Keep track of your assets effectively

Building a source of passive income originates from the desire to become more efficient. Projects of passive income may need a different amount of attention, some monthly, weekly and others annually. In the same way that you set milestones, you need also to set reminders and notes so that when you have to recheck it, you'll know where you left it off.

Set aside time to look at your investments and don't focus so much on results. Sometimes balance is crucial.

## Measure the success of your investment

The criteria of success define the major steps that you need to follow to fulfill the goals of passive income, and progress can be determined via concrete points. These measures are vital for you to be aware that the goal is achievable and is within the ability of everyone. For you to measure the success of your endeavors, compute the total amount of passive income created, and the total percent of your expenses paid for a given project. Think about the effects and the influence created, and the time or energy spent your project. Examine the returns and maximize them, the best passive income portfolio develops with time.

**Should you scale or not to scale**

Once you have fulfilled your goal, and now you have a great source of passive income. Certain investors on this level may decide to scale by cloning their passive income asset different times to replicate their passive income stream. While this is a common approach, and half the work is completed, sometimes a steady and constant income is a better idea.

# Chapter 2: Proven PIG Models

*(PIG = Passive Income Generators)*

## Real estate

Real estate has generated a lot of wealth than any other industry. As a result, millennials have started to invest in real estate in large numbers. Individuals between the age of 36 years and younger make up for the largest group of real estate buyers over the last four years, based on the National Association of Realtors.

There's no question that the following age group has discovered the power that real estate investment can generate.

When getting started in real estate investment as a form of passive income, you need to understand the burdens that loans create. Therefore, it's important to develop a plan for how you want to manage your finances in the right way. Once you avoid accumulating extra credit card debt and so forth, you can swing into action to begin paying down debts as soon as possible. The less debt you have, the more real estate you can buy.

Start by setting aside a small size of each paycheck. Based on the size of your salary, it could be as much as 40% or even as little as 20%. But, if you get into the habit of setting aside the same amount of cash every week, then you'll know how to buy a home very soon.

**Real Estate Investing**

Being a real estate investors will give you total freedom to create generational wealth or smaller amounts for more freedom, the sky is literally the limit.

Today, the most common ways to crate cash flow and wealth from real estate investing are the following

**Investing in rental properties:**

- Low income homes (East entry point, cheaper and more profitable but higher management)

- Expensive suburban homes (much more expensive, lower ROI and cash flow, higher demand from tenants, easier to manage)

- Apartments and commercial properties.(Institutional cash flow, partners, large equity farming, huge cash flows and management can be outsourced to professional companies)

**Flipping Homes as passive income generator:**

- Because of technology you can actually automate this business. Using Internet marketing to create your leads and managing them. Since most of the business is all about marketing, this will be the core activities in flipping

- Wholesale flipping (Easiest point of entry, you can get private money lenders to back you locally, you need none of your own cash, you can make large lump sums of cash very fast. This business is mostly marketing and can be automated on a small scale locally).

We think this is the best passive income generator for new investors, since all you have to do UPFRONT is create a good local investor buyers' list and establish some websites and low-budget marketing to attract and convert motivated sellers automatically. Believe me when I tell you that most eyeballs on online now, so when a motivated seller wants to sell NOW, they don't go looking for that "WE BUY HOMES" post card they got in the mail 2 months ago, they go right to Google and type "sell house fast for cash" in the search bar, and if you have a website and show up, you get the lead. This business can be really fun because you can realistically create a $100,000 to $500,000 a year business part time.

- Retail Flipping (Buying retail homes and remodeling them to resell at maximum market price to home-owners. This business is the most difficult and is not recommended for new comers to real estate. There is a significant amount of time and capital that goes into rehabbing a nice single family home or any property for that matter correctly and managing and delegating contractors.

- REIT's (The most passive form of real estate investing would be to purchase REIT stock online. Dividend returns are usually low unless you have significant capital to invest, so this is not really a life-changer income, but can be good for inflation-hedging on your savings, since bank rates are still under 1%

- Real Estate Agent (this actually is not a bad choice for the current market [2019] if you know how to do marketing. Marketing is the key thing to automate if you have not figured this out yet. This can still be a job upfront though but many successful  agents figure out ways to dominate a zip code or 2 in their local market and then automate it by attracting a team of 1-3 agents under them to do all the grunt work. All you have to do is establish and maintain the lead generation system [Facebook page, ads, SEO, website blog, etc.] You can realistically create a passive $80,000 to $150,000 per year niche agency business this way!)

## How to automate your real estate business?

Once you launch your real estate market, the next thing is to think about how you can automate your passive income stream. Real estate is a market that is ready for a major technological change. Whatever that is possible for automation should be automated. When you begin to think about how you can automate your real estate, the first thing that you need to try and figure out are the processes that you can automate. Automation will profoundly reduce the time on processes and generate resources to the required areas and allow you to stay ahead of the market and your competitors. Below are areas that you need to automate in your real estate investment.

### 1. Business Processes and Automated workflows

An average day in the life of a real estate agent is spent filling, submitting and completing real estate documents, organizing appointments, meetings, open houses, creating budgets for weekly, monthly, quarterly and yearly operations. In addition, there's also managing client emails and databases.

Since these tasks are repetitive, they make the best automation candidates. The daily tasks are overwhelming, especially when you do it manually. Additionally, it takes a massive amount of time. However, with automation software, it can save time and resources.

## 2. Automating marketing

Real estate is a very competitive market and missing one small step can make everything worse. The market has a large number of leads at any time that is usually not utilized. It's a big problem for agents to regularly follow up with each potential client. A marketing automation software can begin with gathering some of these leads and saving the information in a database. The more people registered in the sales funnel, the higher the chance for conversion and sales. Once the leads are collected, it can be channeled and segmented into the required lists, personalize them and send instant emails and reminders to clients. The software can send emails, newsletters, text messages to ensure that interested clients are notified. That way, it creates more opportunities to drive new business and engagement. Marketing can be a time-consuming practice, but when you have the right tools, the entire process becomes easier.

## 3. Management of Property

Attempting to create a balance between maintaining properties, coordinating with other project players, and constantly communicating with clients can be a difficult task that may end up generating a high-stress level for the agents. Automating property management is an important feature if you want to achieve success in the real estate business. Having a collaborative software that focuses on new homes and new renovation, can optimize most tasks without wasting time and money.

## 4. Accounting and financial automating

Fiddling financial statements, accounts payable, transactions and receivable is far from easy. We aren't in a new modern era where you're not supposed to be stuck with manual paperwork when dealing with payments and transactions. Scanning through piles of paperwork or rushing to a post-office because an invoice got lost is a thing of the past. Automating the entire process requires a centralized system for end-to-end managing and streamlining the payment means. With the presence of financial management automation, buying orders generated in the system can be monitored and sent for approval. Automating the payment and financial process means that it's possible to target respective people in real-time.

## 5. Automation of field inspection

Quality home assessment can reveal important information about the status of the home and its systems. A poor quality check may cause a client to reject an offer. Scheduling inspections, collecting data manually, and analyzing pictures to prepare reports and certificates is something common across real estate firms. When you automate some of these inspections, you tend to assist the property manager and the field inspectors. Properties can be prepared for inspection ahead of time and bookings can happen directly from clients.

Once each inspection request is tracked, the system can then match the right field inspectors and hence bring effortless management and intelligence into the process. Reports can then be completed on-site faster using pre-available templates, easy image upload features, and checklists. Edit reports and produce professional reports in a click. Automating indoor and outdoor field inspection can limit manual errors and cut down the entire report delivery time without affecting the quality.

## How to control the real estate business using automation and referrals?

In the real estate sector, both organization and doing a follow up are critical to success. Whether you are working as a single agent controlling multiple deals or a broker who is part of a large team, usually the biggest challenge is getting real estate customers.

The most successful real estate professionals that run it as a passive income have great skills and talent in the field of personal interaction and human relation. When a reputable agent connects directly with their client, the relationship becomes stronger.

### Getting leads in the real estate business

Most clients and brokers know that at any given moment, there is a huge amount of leads that aren't optimized. For instance, some real estate leads who came through a web lead generation technology, or repeat sellers/buyers never get a follow-up, or it is days later!

The challenge is, it's hard for agents to regularly and accurately monitor every prospective sale promptly. Agents do have an ever-growing sphere of influence and will continuously add to their past client database.

They have a difficult task of separating the motivated internet leads from the ones who are curious about the price of neighbor's house or attempt to plan for a future home purchase in 2025.

For most agents, the most significant gap falls within the prospects who ask and don't receive a follow-up, so they return to their devices and phones and call a different agent on another listing.

**Real estate market automation**

When you enter the marketing automation, each lead receives a funneled to the right follow-up sequence, which also has reminders for the agent to try to contact the lead.

Real estate may require a vast level of negotiation, title representatives, face time with clients, and home inspectors. Through the application of automated technology, a busy agent can be present in different places at the same time. The marketing automation software can provide educational emails, text messages, and reminders to interested leads while the agent is showing a home.

Most agents have learned or at least involved the application of social media to get leads. Displaying homeowners holding the keys to their new home on social media sites improves marketing.

## Segment your real estate customers

Audience segmentation is critical. A robust CRM software will allow the agent to tag customers by their category so that they can get emails relevant to their status.

For example, when a client comes through as a buyer lead, it's possible that they are looking for a home to buy. There a few buyer leads who are searching to purchase a home in a short-term, and some could be six to twelve months from purchase. It is important to be at the forefront of those leads because it may require credit repair services, market updates, and loan approval during that period.

The same can be considered of sellers. Some are willing to list their homes ASAP, and some sellers have a particular listing date in their mind. Most places are saturated with agents and competition is fierce. If an agent has multiple clients who have a few months out from a transaction, it's critical that these clients are placed in a time-frame based so that they can maintain the client and agent connection.

## Getting real estate referrals

Realtors have always depended on referrals from past clients, but even more, now that it was initially, real estate referrals are the way to increase your customers base. Most realtors have discovered that many of their sales during the recession has come from people who passed their name on to family and friends.

## Wholesaling in real estate

Wholesaling in real estate occurs when a real estate wholesaler places a distressed home under contract with the aim to allocate the contract to a different buyer. The wholesaler doesn't plan to sell the property or fix it up, but they market the home to prospective buyers for a much better price than they have the property under contract for.

## How to wholesale real estate as a passive income

Wholesaling a real estate property is a short term investing method. Some people tend to confuse it with flipping and fixing, but there are specific differences. Wholesaling is profitable when you want to dive into real estate but don't have a lot of capital. However, the drawbacks of wholesaling can include complicated contracts and confusion about its legality.

If you want to wholesale a real estate, below are the steps to follow:

## 1. Identify a distressed property to wholesale

This is the first step that you need to do. A distressed property is the best suited for wholesaling because it is possible to buy under market value. A distressed property refers to property types in disrepair or one in which the owner is motivated to sell it quickly. By identifying a distressed property will allow you to sell the property higher than what you spend to put it under contract.

Given that part of the exciting feature of wholesaling a real estate is the low capital requirements, newbies to wholesaling a real estate will generally look for free or affordable means to locate a distressed property. Seasoned investors will employ different methods to identify a distressed property, which we shall look later on. Some of the sources for searching for a distressed property include individually created real estate marketing systems, online real estate auction and listing sites, real estate investment groups, and using the services of assistants locally.

## Real estate wholesale groups and real estate investment groups

These sources are organized meetings between the professionals in real estate and investors. They act as a great chance for new wholesalers to connect with real estate agents, contractors, title companies, and appraisers. You may come across partners, lead sources, and even mentors.

These sources will send out emails every week with available properties for sale. The following information can help if you know what it purchased and sold, and how much they're selling for, and the kind of neighborhood that has inventory. This particular information will be useful later on when you apply it to your own wholesaling venture. The properties listed in the email may frequently come from Realtors, but a majority are properties that distressed sellers who have turned over to wholesalers to sell rapidly.

You can get local real estate groups by conducting a quick google search, participate in a Meetup group in your town, or join a Facebook group. You can also contact your local chamber of Commerce and request them if they have any upcoming real estate investor meetings.

## Real estate sites

Real estate sites are the best places to locate distressed properties that are market driven, but again you need to know which ones to search for. You want to make use of sites where motivated sellers can post their own properties

You can look for these motivated sellers plus their distressed properties by searching on sites like Zillow, HomesByOwner, craigslist, and FSBO, Auction.com, HomePath, HomeSteps HudHomeStore, and your local county public Trustee Sale or Sherrif Sales.

When you use public consumer sites, just type in the city or location you're searching for and use keywords in your searches. Keywords will scale down the search so that you can find the most motivated sellers, thus the best deals. Examples of popular keywords include:

- Must sell

- Motivated seller

- Fixer upper

- Estate sale

- Distressed property

## Hire a Property Scouter

This is a common and affordable method used to identify a distressed property. In this method, you hire an assistant to help you locate a distressed property. This person will search for properties that you can wholesale. They will look for these deals by scanning neighborhoods, knocking on doors and cold calling homeowners.

This assistant will not work as an hourly employee and won't be paid up front. However, they will only receive payment when you buy one of the properties that they identified, and it goes to settlement. The real estate industry term for this kind of assistant is a bird dog. The name comes from the dog that likes to hunt for birds, the same way the assistant hunts for property deals.

## Other methods of looking for distressed properties

Once you have completed a few real estate wholesale deals, it is now time to try out different means of finding distressed properties. Three common methods comprise placing bandit signs, working with a realtor, and mailing flyers.

These methods require time and some upfront capital. You will need to assign a thousand dollars to receive bandit signs and put up. The following signs are created to attract home sellers who want to sell their home for whatever reason and decide not to go the traditional way of involving a realtor.

By creating and mailing out letters, postcards, and flyers, you tend to encourage distressed sellers to get in touch with you. For this strategy to become active, you must know who to send them to. You can choose to purchase online mailing lists, or even apply a direct mailing service. This method can be expensive but still works if you conduct it on an automated long term consistent strategy, for example:

Sending out 500 postcards a month to a targeted property owner list in a specific zip code where you have a higher chance of getting a motivated seller calling you that will work for your real estate business model.

Another method that is mostly ignored is finding probate court documents for recently acquired property, but remember ; most realtors aren't comfortable with the wholesale process. That is why it is better to use a realtor who is also a realtor or receive a referral from different real estate wholesaler. The commission of the realtors will have to be factored into the buying price of the home too.

Realtors like to steer clear of the wholesalers because they like to use their own contracts, and they feel comfortable with the standard contract that they're already familiar with. Realtors want to show good faith when they made an offer and given than wholesalers don't want to use their own money, they always skip this step.

Realtors don't feel secure when they assign contracts because the property is being sold twice and the homeowner doesn't know this.

## 2. Create an offer and allow the owner to move on

Once you've located property with the right deal and it is time to talk with the property owner to sell the property to you and authorize the contract. This step is critical because it will help you to protect the properties to wholesale and generate profit.

### Look for the owner

When you go to meet the owner, it is important to do it carefully. Because a wholesaler is not a traditional real estate professional, they will need to win the trust of the homeowner before proceeding. This can be achieved by being courteous, professional and on-time when about to meet the owner. Now here is where many newbies screw up, they think they have to persuade and beg the seller to take their low offer.

Your marketing system has to be set up to attract and act on only motivated sellers, ones that will easily and quickly accept your low offer. They are out there, in all market phases. You are going to get tire kickers responding to your ads, and you have to weed them out upfront or over the phone before investing any time in seeing their property or even writing an offer.

### 3. Have a title company, contractor and appraiser in your contacts

A real estate wholesaler will require a title company, appraiser and contractor on their team. These experts add a level of professionalism to your team and assist your wholesale transaction in the running smoothly. Each profession will save you time and money in the long run.

The appraiser that you work with can appear on short notice and send you an appraisal for the property you want to wholesale. This will make sure that you pay the correct price for the property and have a chance at the price to resell the contract and make some profit. An experienced buyer will also ask for the appraisal before moving forward to purchase the property.

When you have a title company, it will verify that the buyer is purchasing a legitimate piece of real estate. They search for the property to identify whether there are any liens on it. The title company will be applied at settlement, and they will require to be investor friendly. This means that they have to be comfortable to handle assigned contracts.

### Who wholesaling property is right for

Wholesaling is the best for people who want to dive into real estate but don't have the financial means. It is also the best for people who know how to look for distressed properties, are investigative, love analyzing and have a strong god people skills (You do have to know how to talk to sellers). Wholesaling will consume most of the time, but it can generate massive rewards when it is done correctly.

For one to get started in the real estate wholesaling business, you have to be ready to do some research. You will need to find real estate investor groups that you can get some advice. You will also require to set aside time to look for distressed properties and motivate sellers. Lastly, you will need to be familiar with the wholesaling contracts.

If you want to interact with new people, have a passion for real estate and strong communication skill, you can consider real estate wholesaling. For most individuals, it is their first launch into real estate. The reason is that it doesn't require to have a real estate license or any other educational need. Compared to other real estate fields, it requires the least initial capital. That makes it the best for passive income. As you continue to learn wholesale real estate, you will know whether it's going to work out for you or not. There are many gray areas, and it will need a lot of time to find the best properties and buyers to purchase them. Once you engage in a few deals, you'll be familiar with the contracts, the process of marketing, and how to identify distressed properties. By having this knowledge, you will have the confidence you need to succeed in the competitive industry.

## Residential rentals

Everybody's dream is to make money while doing sleeping, or relaxing at home. Well, for some it looks impossible, but that is not the case. You can always choose to invest in residential properties as a means of earning passive income investment to fulfill this dream.

Making passive income is possible, and everybody can realize that dream. When it comes to the best passive income investments, rental properties are one that you should not miss to try out.

## So what is so good about rental properties as a means of passive income investment?

There are several reasons why rental properties are the best passive income investment. Here are some of the most key reasons:

## Rental income

The best thing about rental properties is that they deliver a stable income. What is better than receiving a check every month? But at this stage, you will need to concentrate on the Cashflow. What you want, especially is a positive Cashflow property. Thus, for you to have a positive cash flow, you need to make sure that you need to be sure that you invest in the right rental property that will generate profit.

There are two forms of real estate properties in the market: the positively driven properties and negatively driven properties. In general, the first one generates a positive Cashflow, whereas the second a negative Cashflow. Just be sure that you always select positively driven properties, especially when you're starting out in real estate. There is no need to invest in a negative Cashflow when your main goal is to make money in real estate.

To ensure that you always choose properties that will generate a positive Cashflow, you need to learn to use a rental property calculator. This real estate analytic tool will produce real magic in your property choice. What it merely does is that carriers out real estate market analysis and investment property analysis. The following analysis comprises determining the cap rate, the rental income, and cash on return. Naturally, you can identify whether a rental property is valuable by using a rental property calculator. You can also use it to determine the profits or even losses of your rental property.

**You get to participate**

By not getting actively involved causes rental properties to be one of the best passive income investments in real estate. As an investor in real estate, you need to know that rental properties have a lot of responsibilities. Luckily for you, there different management firms that will be ready to help you in some of the tasks.

Management of property is a form of investment management that you must have in this case. Professional management property companies will handle your properties daily tasks. The following tasks comprise of rent collection, handling your tenants, and maintaining rental records. They will also deal with the legal issues of your rental properties.

However, you need to remember that some property management fees are charged. That is, probably the only drawback of passive income investment in real estate. You need to include these fees to the property expenses and expect them to drop your cash flow. But, this doesn't mean that you will have nothing. Keep in mind that the role of a property manager is to optimize the rental income while making sure that your expenses are down. So, no need to worry about that.

**Part-time investment**

Passive income you earn through rental properties give you the ability to invest part time. This means that passive real estate investors can still concentrate on their normal jobs, while also earning money from their rental properties. For this one, you will need to hire contractors and property management to work on your behalf.

In this case, by investing in rental properties, it will generate an extra income without much effort. Remember, though, that when you invest part time while you allow property managers to handle your property doesn't mean you begin to relax.

Ensure that you are always current with whatever is happening in your business.

## Out of state investing

Another option that presents itself when you take part in passive income investments in rental properties is the out of state investing. Whichever option you choose, you will need to hire professional property management, and so, why not get started with out of state investing?

Search for the best ROI locations in other states and ensure that you purchase the correct property. Not only are there a lot of profitable in the Rust Belt areas and SouthEast locations but also you can select different real estate investment approaches. You can decide to select short-term rentals. This is also a profitable investment method. Just look for the best locations for your goals and go with it.

You can also decide to invest in traditional rentals. It is up to you. But if you choose to invest in both strategies, it will provide you with the best opportunity to diversify an investment portfolio and eliminate risks as much as you can.

## Retail Flipping

If you want to make the most amount of money in residential real estate, then you need to consider flipping houses. The only challenge is that most people have wrong perceptions about flipping houses. Some think that to flip a house you must have huge capital, or that it is like what we see on popular TV shows about flipping homes.

Finding capital to flip homes is not a problem in today's markets. The amount of private wealth looking for ROI is massive right now, actually the demand for investment currently exceeds available investments, so that is in your favor.

Generating income flipping houses isn't just an exactly passive, but it can be a super profitable side hustle if you can do 2-3 deals a year part time also a profitable strategy when you know what you're doing.

Investors have made a lot of money using this approach. Here's exactly what you need to know and do to start earning money flipping houses. First, you must know the geographic location of the land. You must know the market forces and the playing ground, and then from here, you can take advantage of it.

Your main goal is to look for a distressed seller and you have to know the retail home values in your area. On the other hand, a cash buyer who will allow you to close the transaction quickly and manage to turn around and sell your property fast. And, finally, you want to make a profit after the process.

So how can you do that very fast? You need to identify the correct buyers. This means you have to look for investors. If you know a few rich guys or you have friends with people who are already investing in the real estate market, then that is great. If you don't have any, go to the web and do some research. There are different marketing techniques that you can apply to make sure that you target the right buyers. You can opt to create a complete sales funnel, or even run a Facebook ad. You can also do a webinar.

*However, if you want to save yourself time, then you should scan through records of the county. Inside, you'll find a gold mine of data. A large amount of information is sitting there waiting to be selected. So you just need to analyze the county records for all the transactions and identify the correct buyers. This will take some effort and time, but it's the simplest method to make money.*

It's going to be a waste of time to look for distressed and motivated sellers when you don't have cash buyers ready and cultivated (if you are wholesaling). The only method that you can flip the contract is when you have both parties lined up.

**For retail flipping**, you really do not need to look for buyers, because you are not selling to Investors, you will be selling to local home buyers that will pay top dollar because they are getting financing. Generally, you will place the home on the MLS with an agent when you are done with the rehab, this will expose it to everyone looking for a home in that market, and all associated consumer sites like Zillow, Trulia, Redfin, Realtor.com, Etc. The 80/20 most profitable taks in retail flipping is FINDING A GOOD DEAL or a house that has equity after your remodel so you can make a profit. Most investor in most amrkets make a profit of $30,000 to $150,000 per home for retail flipping. So this is why you can make a nice "passive" side income by doing only 2-3 a year. It is not hard to find a private money partner in your local market to get the money for this, and even better if you have the cash then it's just you, or..if you own a home free and clear, try to get a home equity line of credit. Bb creative, and remember that real estate investing works in EVERY market cycle, don't forget that.

Simple steps:

1. Pick the right market

2. Choose the right property

3. Make the right offer price – your profit is always made in your buy price

4. Identify the right buyers

5. Identify the right sellers

**Other notes:**

- Real estate investment income can be passive if run exclusively online as a wholesale operation – converting seller leads and flipping fast to cash investor buyers. You can do this nationwide also.

- Flipping retail properties is more of a side hustle than a passive income, but has tremendous profit potential, even with only 3 deals a year you can replace your job income. Many local investors do this, you can find them in every city, find one and offer them lunch for some tips and guidance.

- Real estate agency income can be passive if you work really hard upfront for several months, focus on a niche market, and are really good at setting up Internet marketing systems and lead follow up, in addition to acquiring team mates to do the grunt work. This has been done many time over but won't really be passive until you can establish these system upfront and create your own little team.

# Affiliate Marketing

Affiliate marketing is another great proven way to make passive income. When most people hear about passive income, they only think about receiving a one-time commission. But that is not the case. In fact, affiliate marketing has many different alternatives.

It is possible to build a recurring, passive income stream from affiliate marketing as long as you find the right vendors. However, this doesn't mean that you should only aim to market companies or even products that only generate a one-time sale.

If a given product helps your readers, then promote it. Your goal should always be to assist your readers and improve their lives. If you can focus your time and energy on growing your passive income, while at the same time being helpful to your readers, then why not do it?

It doesn't matter how to look at the following idea; it is possible through affiliate marketing to generate recurring income for life. The current digital marketing system operates on a revenue sharing system. Affiliate marketers sell a different product or service and receive a commission on the number of sales they generate.

If implemented correctly, affiliate marketing can allow a person to make a constant flow of passive income. You will come across thousands of online blogs that market affiliate marketing as getting rich quick scheme, but that is far from the truth.

To become successful as an affiliate, you need to be dedicated and ready to work hard. From picking the correct products to maintaining blogs, there is so much work that you need to do.

However, there are different methods that you can optimize your recurrent income with affiliate marketing.

**Affiliate programs are divided into two categories:**

1.  One-time commission model

2.  Recurring commission model

**One-time commission model**

It's the easiest model. You simply refer a product through an online publishing platform. If any of your audience purchases the product, you receive a fixed commission for that. In this model, more referrals are equal to more commission.

**Recurring commission model**

This is the best model to make recurring income. Recurring affiliate programs don't just pay based conversion alone but also pay each month as long as the user maintains the subscription.

This can be a good strategy to increase your recurring income. You receive your monthly share without doing a lot of work, as long as the subscription continues. This system generally works for any digital product or even service like web hosting, and online courses.

## ClickBank

Clickbank program is among the first online programs. Affiliate marketing using ClickBank is quite common nowadays. In fact, this is one of the top companies that you should use to promote a product.

The effectiveness and accessibility of this program make it popular. If you didn't know, the ClickBank affiliate program gives you the ability to market products digitally.

However, Clickbank affiliate marketing works in two ways. First, as a vendor, you need to ensure that you pay a commission to the people who promote your product. If you are going to place the affiliate ads on your page, then you must create quality content that can grab the attention of readers and also market products that you have chosen.

Whatever you earn is directly dependent on the products that you can promote and the total number of clicks that is equivalent to the amount of purchase.

As such, the total number of buys will translate the clicks into possible earnings.

This is the premise which companies like ClickBank apply. In other words, it is the driving formulae for any affiliate marketing strategy.

However, to make money from Clickbank doesn't happen so quickly. In most cases, once you register for ClickBank, you'll start looking at some low standard products and begin to wonder how you can generate money from it. Sometimes it will happen that you will keep trying for even months. The problem with the ClickBank affiliate program is the way to make a profit.

This simply means that ClickBank affiliate marketing is not as easy as it sounds. Although you need to gain practice and harness your skills, you also need to be shrewd when selecting products. If you fail to choose the right products to market, then your whole program will fail.

For that reason, if you're targeting ClickBank program as an alternative source of income, it is important to come up with a well thought out plan.

Not only is it advantageous to familiarize with the effects of the program correctly, but also how you should run it effectively to optimize your gains.

You need to involve yourself in deep research of the different provisions of the affiliate program and look at the opportunities to improve the gains and boost the earnings.

Keep in mind that the content of the website you're placing the ads also counts a lot.

## Other CPA Networks

Making money in CPA networks isn't that hard as some people think. This is an industry within the affiliate network. CPA is a process that will allow you to make money from someone doing a specific action such as signing up for an offer, submitting emails, installing an application and many more.

## How CPA works

The best thing about CPA is that you don't necessarily need to sell any product or service. But you will make money from doing some action through a website.

Below is a list of the top CPA Network that you can consider when you want to join a CPA network. Keep a close watch on the offers, support systems, and commission payouts. If you want to get the best CPA networks, then you should make an effort to join these:

### 1. Peerfly

This is a genuine, trusted and popular network used by publishers because of its excellent team management. It is friendly and pays on time. The network provides a wide variety of niche markets without any country limitation. By using their referral program, you can get a 5% commission on every referral for a lifetime.

The average rate of conversion is about 8%. Also, it offers weekly payments with the least payout of $50 through Paypal, Postal Check, and Payoneer.

## 2. CPAlead

This network has all types of complex solutions to change traffic into a premium content for a profitable revenue stream such as a monetized digital widget. The CPA lead network is said to be the best because of compliance assurance and fault prevention.

## 3. Maxbounty

This was developed with, and the goal of being the best money remitter and every payment is completed before the scheduled time.

It also offers money in different currencies. MaxBounty is the best option to involve in a highly converting and top paying advertising offer. You can get the relevant offers in just a second. The minimum payout for Maxbounty is $50.

## 4. Clickbooth

If you like to advertise, Clickbooth offers you the right opportunity to get prospective customers by looking in the database for exclusive affiliates.

The company has an active affiliate review process that aims to protect the integrity of intellectual property advertisers.

If you are an advertiser, Clickbooth will deliver the best offers on your website. The mix of Clickbooth ads with content are combined it easy to be found by search engines.

### 5. Convert2Media

This network has over 1000 advertisers. The company focuses most on publishers. The payment methods of convert2media include Bank wire, Paypal and check with the least payout of $100.

### 6. OfferVault
## Amazon affiliate marketing

If you are looking to establishing a passive income stream, then Amazon affiliate marketing can be the best way to earn some money from monetizing your blog. By referring products for sale for Amazon, you'll collect a huge commission that ranges from 1% to 10% of the sale price for items your readers to buy during the session they begin to come from your website.

# Chapter 3: Information Products

If you're starting in passive income, building information products are the best way to generate money online. Below are some of the advantages of creating an information business.

- **Easy to start:** Compared to the traditional business style of selling physical products, you don't need to manage an inventory and store physical products. No need to recruit staffs or deal with suppliers, salespeople, manufacturers, and shippers. With only a laptop, you can begin to improve your expertise and pick a digital product type to work on.

- **Easy to build:** You can simply save your word document as a PDF and begin to sell it as an eBook on Amazon, website, Apple iBook and many other retailers.

- **Little or no cost:** It's a low –risk business model. It costs very little to create an informational product.

- **Sell Internationally:** You are not limited to only selling it to your local market. You can also target your audience across the world. And begin to sell the product to the whole world.

- **Great sources of passive income:** Once you build your product, you can generate passive income by selling it repeatedly. You can decide to market and ensure that the content remains up to date, but you don't need to involve yourself in the selling process.

Like any other business, selling informational products comes with its own challenges. Some of the drawbacks include:

- **It calls for a lot of upfront active work.** It requires enough time to build quality information products.

- **Low selling price.** This is very common for those dealing with ebooks. The days when an eBook would cost $39, $73 and even $199 have kind of passed. Today, readers can still get the same quality information from $2.99 to $9.99 on Kindle. If you choose to join the Amazon Kindle Unlimited Program, you'll be paid for each page read, and it's less than $0.0005 per page. You can do the math.

**Types of informational products you can create**

With the expansion of technology, you can now monetize your expertise and knowledge online. There is a lot of information available online. People can purchase what they want easily with just a touch of a button.

*There are different types of products that you can sell online. Let's get started:*

# Drop shipping physical products

There is no argument that passive income is something that everyone wishes to achieve. The thought of being able to build a business and have it generate money every day with little effort put sounds exciting, but most people don't know how to get started.

## So, what is drop shipping?

It is the first thing that you need to know. Drop shipping is a method that builds a supply chain model that will let the retailer stop keeping any stock. All orders will be transferred directly to the wholesaler, and they will ship the items or goods to the customer directly.

## Basics of drop shipping

There are different things that you need to pay attention to before you can earn money from drop shipping. You will learn some of the basics that will help you to begin on the right track. Remember that these are important guidelines and they are crucial if you want to realize positive results.

## Choose the right product to sell

Drop shipping is a powerful method to earn passive income, but you need to build your business before you can see the results. Pick the correct product to make sure that conversions based on your target audience go hand in hand.

## Develop a professional website

There is no point to spend a fortune to develop a site anymore. Nowadays, anyone can do it without any strong coding and programming by taking advantage of the content management systems such as WordPress. The significance and value of your website is critical because it will act as the source that will publish your content. Next, you can share the same content on various social media platforms and websites.

## Look for the correct supplier

Your supplier is going to handle the products to the doorsteps of every single customer, and this will be done on your behalf. This is one of the primary reasons why you deserve to get someone who is going to be responsible and who knows how to do the job effectively.

## Remain consistent with your marketing efforts

Before you can make some passive income from drop shipping, you will need to spend some good time working hard on building your audience. You can do this by marketing your products through your blog and social media shares. Remember that converting drop shipping into a job that generates passive income isn't something that happens overnight, but the fruits of your hard work are going to match your commitment.

## Blogging

You have heard about people making money online. But what about starting a blog and making some passive income so that you can quit your 9-5 job and avoid the rat race. This is not about earning $2.47 per month from your hobby. It's about generating hundreds and thousands of dollars every month doing something that you like and are passionate about.

Selling your time for dollars is the worst style to earn a living, but most people do it because they think it is safe. Whether you're looking for freedom or some extra money, starting a blog will help you make real money online which will open new doors you didn't think were there.

Blogging is a great way to just start, writing and researching about things that you LIKE and have a serious interest in.

## Authoritative blogging

An authority blog is one that delivers expert opinions and information about specific topics in a selected niche. It's a type of blog that has in-depth and researched content than other blogs in the same niche. This particular content is referred to as authority content. This section will help you to understand authority content and how you can become authoritative in your industry.

There are various steps that you will learn to develop a better understanding of this topic. The first and most crucial step toward creating authority content is becoming an expert. Becoming an expert in a given field will assist you in delivering content and information that your competitors cannot generate. This will also allow you to express yourself confidently and appear trustworthy to your audiences.

Building authority in your industry through your blog and delivering quality content is <u>the best method to attain successful content marketing</u>. It will allow you to get a successful blog even when you don't have a vast audience, and it will assist you in working towards achieving a reputation of an influential blogger that people can trust and follow. This will give you the ability to drive more sales than applying direct methods of advertising.

One strategy that can help you to begin towards building an authority blog in any niche is to start by doing a review of other authority content creators. By researching the best examples of authority content delivery and researching competitors can provide valuable insight into their strategies that make their authority content successful. You need to carefully evaluate the style of their writing, and the jargon they use. Looking at their favorite blog posts, and taking some notes is the best way to begin.

This can also generate valuable information about selecting the best profitable niche. Some topics are more interactive and more popular than others. Identify what's trending, what makes people interested and identify specific topics in your selected niche. By starting with a small audience and targeting topics is a significant strategy into building authority and trust.

## Niche blogging

Starting a blog is both exciting and a bit scary.

Interesting because it's a brand new venture that has endless opportunities. Many people begin blogs with the goal of turning it into a career so that they can schedule and free themselves from the corporate world. We dream about a happy life away from the 9-5 office job.

Blogging sounds scary because there are numerous steps that you need to do before you can launch your blog. This can be somehow confusing. Suppose you make a big mistake right out of the gate?

Don't be afraid; it's not that difficult. In other words, it's not that hard to get started. But you need to know that blogging can be somehow difficult.

## Blog Niche

A blog niche refers to a topic that you can select to write about for a particular group of people. Let's say you want to write about food in general. That can be said to be a vast topic. On the other hand, picking something within the topic of food such as vegan recipes can be said to be a niche.

The reason is that it's better to select a niche instead of a broad topic because the internet has lots of blogs and websites. The competition is huge. And in most cases, broad topic sites belong to big companies with a large advertising budget.

By scaling down your niche, it will allow you to attract an audience that wants to solve a specific problem. When you narrow down your niche, you have a better chance to beat the big guys. Also, you get readers who are loyal than broad topic readers. They return to your site because you have given them something of value that has become relevant in their lives.

**Consultant**

You can also make a passive income as a consultant. But it is not that easy as you may imagine and may fall more under the "side hustle" category. There are endless ways that you can generate passive income from being a consultant though.

First, you must build an inventory of your skills.

List down things that you enjoy doing; What is it that you know you are good at? From here you can move forward to begin a lucrative career in your field.

If you're driven to make money as a consultant, you might consider converting it from a part-time to a full-time job. Whichever way, it is crucial that you focus on how you can generate income from your consultancy, more work means less passive income.

As a consultant, you can choose to earn your income on an hourly rate. This means you will charge your clients on an hourly rate. To ensure that you remain successful, you must create a consulting fee. Being a consultant requires a lot of hard work and risk. As a result, your payment should reflect your work.

**Software-as-a-service**

If you know about programming and software development, why not use it make money passively?

The Software as a service approach has continued to gain traction across all parts of the world, and for a good reason. Also known as a hosted software or on-demand software, SaaS beats traditional software installation and management methods by applying cloud-based applications through the internet. With SaaS, service providers can remove the burden of security, and performance.

Organizations of different shapes and sizes continue to embrace the SaaS philosophy as an alternative option to on-premises software and hardware deployment.

SaaS is well suited for a small business. Rather than investing in extra house server capacity, companies can adjust their Software as a service subscription on a monthly plan, scaling consumption and project based on demands and other types of valuables.

## Amazon FBA

Every digital worker loves the idea of earning money by working less. This has caused a tremendous stir among young entrepreneurs in affiliate marketing.

The amazon marketplace is always overlooked and has a lot of opportunities for one to make some reasonable amount of passive income.

The Amazon FBA is one of the best means to sell products without worrying about sales or even shipping. What you only need to do is to list the product, and ship it to Amazon store.

Once your product arrives at the Amazon store, your product is kept in the Amazon warehouse. When a sale is done, the product is delivered to the customer on your behalf by Amazon.

Keep in mind that this is not a get-rich-quick-scheme. To succeed, you will need to dedicate some hours and energy into the venture. Your most significant effort is to research and ship products to Amazon.

To purchase the products, you must have some capital. The amount of money that you want to begin with is your own choice.

## Overview of how the FBA process operates

Amazon will handle everything as long as they receive your product. The Amazon FBA process is simple:

- Research products that you want to sell on Amazon.

- Purchase the products from a supplier or wholesale.

- Register for an Amazon FBA account and start to create your listings.

- Package and brand your product.

- Ship the product to Amazon

- Sit back and wait for sales to flow in.

This may appear as a lot of work, but once you can ship the product to the fulfillment center, then your most significant task is over.

## Costs to start selling

Don't confuse this with drop shipping. Before you start to sell on FBA, it is essential to have some capital. This capital will allow you to buy a physical inventory, and then pay the costs of shipping. Also, you will also need to pay for the Amazon warehouse fee, referral fee, and subscription fees.

Once you list a product, you can make use of the FBA calculator to compute the exact cost of the service fees.

## Amazon Kindle books

Earning passive income from Amazon kindle requires that you create an eBook. Yes, you can write a book and sell it for money. Amazon Kindle publishing is so easy because there is no restriction to entry. Thus, you can write something in Google docs, look for a designer to create a cover for you on Fiver. Next, look for someone to format it for Amazon Kindle, and then you can upload your Kindle author account. If you have a decent $60 podcasting mic, then you can decide to record the audio version of your book, which tends to sell even better. The secret to success with Amazon Kindle involves:

- Find a good editor.

- Get a great cover design and formatting.

- Learn how to market your book

**Once you get a book into the Kindle marketplace, you can sell ebook, paperback and Audio versions of it all on autopilot.**

# Domains names

People still buy and sell domains names, this can be like real estate only you are buying a digital asset on online marketplaces, auctions, manually and expired domains. You can build a niche portfolio of domains names and sell them in bundles, or hold for passive CPA cash flow, really, there are no limits, it all about how much upfront work you are willing to put in to get it to the passive stage.

## Flipping domains

Domain flipping is the process of buying a domain name and selling it at a higher cost. This resembles house flipping, where you purchase a house and fix it up to sell at a quick profit. Unlike house flipping, there is nothing you can do with the domain name to increase its value. As a result, the secret to a successful domain flip is to be in the right place at the right time to get the best domain name before it is offered at a premium price. If you are lucky, you'll come across great domain name by looking watching expireds and dropped names every day, and knowing what buyers are buying right now

## Cash parking

Websites that have nothing except an advertisement block and search bar aren't broken, these are parked domains. Domain parking is the process of registering a domain without any service or content connected to the domain name. No landing page, no website, no generation off, or anything

When users stumble a parked website, the webmaster will earn some revenue on a CPC basis for every advertisement click. You may ask yourself, why someone would go to a parked domain?

Well, experts in the domain parking have a few tricks to purchase the correct domain names. Purchasing expired domains or misspelled domains is one of the most popular tricks to get started with domain parking, although these techniques are fading out.

Just like with domain flipping, domain parking requires a person to buy valuable domains that people are going to type into the browser.

However, if you have domain names that are not in use, or you want to experiment for some fun, domain parking could be a smart experiment.

**Flipping websites**

This is the process of buying a website, developing it into a website and acquiring traffic, and then selling it at a higher price. This is similar to property flipping, where a house is bought and fixed, then sold at a higher price. For website flipping, an investor will purchase the website, add value to it, and then sell it at a higher price. This is not easy though and if you want passive income, its best to keep the websites/ domains as income generators.

## Digital freelancing

The increasing connectivity of the digital world has reduced the physical and geographical barriers in most industries. This means that people can work and remain productive wherever they are at any time.

The freelance economy has continued to grow every year as more people are quitting their jobs to become digital freelancers. With a lot of avenues to explore, more and more businesses are searching for freelance digital marketing specialists to assist them in delivering the right projects and campaigns.

As a result, becoming a digital marketing freelancer is definitely a lucrative and flexible option.

## Google AdSense CPM Income

Google AdSense is one of the most natural means to monetize a blog and website content. Once you sign up for an account and is approved, all that you need to do is to create some AdSense code. Insert the code into your website and then start to make money.

The most important thing of any website that wants to generate revenue from Google AdSense is to understand the number of visitors that are required to create a sensible revenue. Until you have a reasonable number of visitors, earnings from AdSense can be meager.

# Stocks and Bonds

### Dividend Stocks

This is one of the easiest means for investors to build a source of passive income because you're getting paid to own them. As the company generates new earnings, part of the profits is paid to investors as a dividend. This money can then be reinvested to buy extra shares or get a cash payment.

Dividends yields can be different from one company to the next, and they can also change from year to year. Investors that aren't sure about the dividend-paying stocks can decide to use the one that fit the dividend aristocrat label.

Other forms of passive securities that require no work

### Treasury Bonds

These are super safe; in fact, bond holders get paid back no matter what.

If you have a deposit account at a bank and the bank goes under, you stand a chance of losing your savings even with FDIC insurance, because what most people do not know is FDIC insurance does not have to pay you back right away, they have up to 15 years and can pay you back in monthly installments as low at $100! Anyone can open a Treasury account online to buy their own government bonds. As of today 4 week T-Bills are yielding 2.35% (Annualized of course)

Other long term super passive equity investments:

- Exchange Traded Funds

- Mutual Funds

- Commodity-based funds

- Hedge Funds

- Private Equity

- REIT's

- Etc.

# Summary

Passive income generation is best suited for the time-constrained individuals. Even super wealthy people are limited by time. Passive income is one great way to avoid time limitations, but it can easily turn into a full time business with major wealth creation possibilities.

There are multiple ways to generate passive income, and we've only looked at a few. Luckily, you can come up with other ideas with a little creative thinking or brainstorming.

If you don't have passive income sources, start adding them today. The sooner you start; the sooner you will build your bank account. The time is going to go by anyways.

If you can create a passive income source that generates even $5 per day, then you'll earn more than $1,800 in the first year. This is a considerable return for part-time work, and can cover the cost of many things, property taxes, car payments, credit card payments, etc.

**Imagine if you had more than three sources like this.**

**How hard do you think it can be to make $5 a day?**

Turn every thought, fact, idea that comes into your mind pay you profit. Make it work and produce for you. Look at things not as they are but as they could be. Don't just be a dreamer, but become a creator and action-taker, in today's digital age, you won't even have to leave your home-office to make this happen.

# Helpful Links and Resources:

https://www.milliondollarwinnie.com/2019/02/05/the-benefits-of-passive-income-and-why-passive-income-is-so-important/

https://www.wanderlustworker.com/what-is-passive-income-and-how-do-you-create-it/

http://www.appleseedpermaculture.com/8-forms-of-capital/

https://medium.com/swlh/how-to-automate-your-real-estate-business-b193ea8ccd6

https://keap.com/infusionsoft/business-success-blog/marketing/automation/how-to-dominate-the-real-estate-industry-with-automation

https://fitsmallbusiness.com/how-to-wholesale-real-estate/

https://www.luckscout.com/clickbank-affiliate-program/

https://www.awefirst.com/top-10-best-cpa-networks/

https://techmasi.com/best-cpa-networks/

https://thinkmaverick.com/make-passive-income-selling-information-products/

http://skillslane.com/drop-shipping-passive-income-generation/

https://www.entrepreneur.com/article/283006]

https://webhostingmedia.net/make-your-blog-authoritative-niche/

https://www.brandbuilders.io/generate-passive-income-fba-amazon/

https://www.hover.com/blog/domain-flipping-definition/

http://websiteflipping.com/

https://digitalmarketinginstitute.com/blog/how-to-become-a-freelance-digital-marketer

https://medium.com/trust-works/money-from-adsense-calculate-how-many-visitors-you-need-fac02363001e